43 Team-building Activities
for Key Stage 1

Gavin Middlewood and
Andrew Debenham

Brilliant
PUBLICATIONS

We hope that you and your pupils enjoy doing the activities in this book. Brilliant Publications publishes many other books for use in primary schools. To find out more details on any of the titles listed below, please log on to our website: www.brilliantpublications.co.uk.

Team Building Activities for Key Stage 2	978-1-903853-57-3
Thinking Strategies for the Successful Classroom 5-7 Year Olds	978-1-905780-03-7
Thinking Strategies for the Successful Classroom 7-9 Year Olds	978-1-905780-04-4
Thinking Strategies for the Successful Classroom 9-11 Year Olds	978-1-905780-05-1
Timely Tasks for Fast Finishers 5-7 Year Olds	978-1-905780-00-6
Timely Tasks for Fast Finishers 7-9 Year Olds	978-1-905780-01-3
Timely Tasks for Fast Finishers 9-11 Year Olds	978-1-905780-02-0
Positively Me – A Self-esteem Programme for Teachers and Pupils	978-1-903853-13-9
Into the Garden of Dreams	978-1-897675-76-2
Smiling Inside, Smiling Outside – Learning to Care for Myself, My Family, My World	978-1-903853-73-3
Brilliant Activities for Gifted and Talented Children	978-1-903853-47-4
Brilliant Activities for Stretching Gifted and Talented Children	978-1-905780-17-4

Published by Brilliant Publications
Unit 10
Sparrow Hall Farm
Edlesborough
Dunstable
Bedfordshire
LU6 2ES, UK

Sales and stock enquiries:
Tel: 01202 712910
Fax: 0845 1309300
E-mail: brilliant@bebc.co.uk
Website: www.brilliantpublications.co.uk

General information enquiries:
Tel: 01525 222292

The name Brilliant Publications and the logo are registered trademarks.

Written by Gavin Middlewood and Andrew Debenham
Illustrated by Pat Murray
Cover designed by Gloss Solutions
Cover photograph by Julie Thatcher

© Text Gavin Middlewood and Andrew Debenham 2009
© Design Brilliant Publications 2009
ISBN 978-1-905780-49-5

First printed and published in the UK in 2009

Contents

Introduction

What are the aims of this book?

This book aims to provide children with the opportunity to develop in a range of social and physical skills. These skills are developed through a series of carefully written lesson plans that have been designed with the busy primary teacher in mind. These activities aim at stimulating pupils' imaginations through a series of exciting problems and scenarios.

Where does this fit into the school curriculum?

PE

Each of the activities aims at developing the Key Stage 1 child in their fundamental movement skills: agility, balance and co-ordination. As well as this, the children will be thinking about when to select these skills and how to apply them.

PSHE

These activities aim to improve the child's social skills with a partner or within a small group. These skills can then be transferred into the classroom and playground environments. Each activity acknowledges the importance of every individual as a valued part of a team. Successful completion of these tasks requires even the most reticent children to become involved. There is also the opportunity for pupils to become more responsible and to take on leadership roles.

43 Team-building Activities for Key Stage 1
© Gavin Middlewood and Andrew Debenham

Setting the adventures

The stories in this book invite the children to take on many different roles, from monkeys serving Wazzoo, the Monkey King, to explorers unearthing treasures in Egypt. Some stories make use of well-known characters, such as Robin Hood, to aid in the construction of the scenario. Others suggest to the children that they find their everyday selves in highly unusual and challenging situations.

In order to assist continuity, and to help some children build a more detailed imaginative context within which to work, a number of the challenges have been set in the fantasy world of Gazaban. Many of the characters in these stories make repeat appearances and, should you choose to use their names, you may find the information below useful.

The good guys

King Rondo: the mighty (hungry) ruler of Gazaban

Prince Larry: King Rondo's son

Princess Wilma: King Rondo's daughter

Pirate Pete: Captain of 'The Golden Parrot'

Long Don Silver: Pirate Pete's first mate

Wizard Zalbo: The king's wizard and defender of Gazaban

The dark side

Zed the Witch: Arch enemy of Zalbo and the whole of Gazaban

The Captain of 'The Black Rat' (no-one knows his name!)

Remember that all stories can be adapted as the teacher feels appropriate for the class and the curriculum content.

The magic bubble

Easy

The evil wicked witch Zed is creating mischief in the magical land of Gazaban. She is turning everyone into a frog. Everyone is hopping mad! You gaze at the green, slimy bodies with webbed feet and decide that you don't want to be a frog. You have nothing against them, but humans seem to have much better lives. Luckily, Zalbo, the friendly wizard, has a spell to protect you from being turned into a frog. With the aid of the frogs, 'The Magic Bubble', will help you to travel through the land of Gazaban to safety. Can you make it across without being turned green?

Focus
Coordination, cooperation
Number in group
3-4
Equipment
Large hoops
Aim
To travel across the playing area by stepping through the hoops positioned by the other group members.

Instructions

1. In each group, one person should be chosen to be the human, whilst the other members become the frogs. The frogs are all given hoops which create 'The Magic Bubble'.

2. The human must attempt to cross the land of Gazaban (the playing area). However, he or she can only move with the protection of 'The Magic Bubble'. This means that the human can only take a step forward if it is through a hoop that is held in front of them by a frog. Humans can only take one step at a time. Frogs are only allowed to move ahead of their human by hopping.

3. Both the humans and the frogs should be reminded that they must take great care when the human passes through the hoop. If the hoop is touched, then 'The Magic Bubble' is burst, and the team must go back to the start.

Extension: Guiding the humans over a bridge (an upturned bench) will require balance and precision from the team.

43 Team-building Activities for Key Stage 1
© Gavin Middlewood and Andrew Debenham

Save the pirates!

You are pirates in the middle of the ocean and your ship, 'The Golden Parrot', is in the middle of a great battle with your enemies, the pirates of 'The Black Rat'. 'Fire! Fire!' cries the captain on board the enemy ship. Suddenly a number of huge cannonballs blast a hole in the end of your ship which, unluckily for you, is just the part that you are standing upon. Splash! You and your best friend, Long Don Silver, fall into the water below. Neither of you have learnt to swim yet but there is a piece of wood that you can stand on next to you. Can you balance together on this piece of wood until your fellow crew members save you?

Focus
Cooperation, balance
Number in group
2
Equipment
Quoits
Aim
To balance upon the quoit, with a partner, for as long as possible.

Instructions

1. Give each pair a piece of wood (quoit) to stand upon. Let them both practise balancing upon it so that they can get used to its shape.

2. The children will need to find a way of balancing themselves on the quoit together. No feet may touch the ocean (the floor around them). They will probably only find room to place one foot each on the quoit.

3. The children need to retain their balance upon the wood for as long as possible. The teacher may set several time challenges, for example, 5, 10 and 20 seconds or maybe longer.

Extension: A small circle of three touching quoits could be used to make a large piece of wood. How many pirates can the children fit on this?

The princess and the puddle

Princess Xania is not just a little bit posh…she is very posh indeed! When she has a bath she bathes in milk and washes her hair with fresh honey. When Princess Blodwyn goes downstairs to breakfast she walks upon rose petals so that her feet do not have to touch the cold, hard floor! Princess Elegentia never goes anywhere without her 15 serving maids. Today the three princesses have come to visit the Prince at the palace where you work. Unfortunately it has been raining all night and there is a massive muddy puddle in front of the door. The red carpet is at the cleaners but can you use the cushions to help the princesses across the enormous puddle?

Focus
Balance, problem-solving
Number in group
3-4
Equipment
Quoits
Aim
To plan where to place the quoits so that a child can cross the playing area without touching the floor.

Instructions

1. Organize the children into groups. Each group needs to choose one child to be the princess. The others will be the servants.

2. The teacher must identify the puddle (the playing area) and explain that the servants must help the princess to cross it without touching the floor.

3. Each group will then be given four velvet cushions (quoits). They must plan where to line these up so that the princess can cross the puddle.

4. The princess must attempt to cross the puddle without touching the floor.

Hint: The cushions should be spread apart evenly so that the princess can reach each one. Some children may spot that they can re-use a cushion once it has been used by moving it on ahead of the princess.

Extensions: Choose another child to be princess, and play again. Teams can be invited to race each other across the puddle in order to win the prince's hand in marriage. The size of the puddle can also be increased. Greater planning skills will be needed!

---

43 Team-building Activities for Key Stage 1
© Gavin Middlewood and Andrew Debenham

Boulder roll

As you return from your school trip to the museum, your coach stops suddenly in the road. You and your classmates get off the coach and see a giant boulder that has fallen from the hill next to the road. Your coach can't go any further. There's no space around it. There's no space under it. And your coach does not have wings! You will need to work with your friends to move the boulder along the road and to push it off the hillside. However, it is very heavy!

Instructions

1. Each group will need a 'road' made out of cones.

2. The group should decide upon an order on which they can touch the boulder (ball) to get it to the end of the road. No pupil can touch the boulder twice in a row as the boulder is very heavy.

3. The children can begin to move the boulder. If the boulder rolls off the road or any pupil touches it twice in a row, the activity must begin again from the start.

Focus
Coordination, communication, cooperation
Number in group
3-4
Equipment
Large balls
Cones
Aim
To move the ball along the road with group members taking one turn at a time to touch the ball.

Hint: Successful groups will plan where the person needs to stand so that they are ready for their touch of the boulder.

Extensions: A road with more twists and turns will require greater care and co-ordination. You could also set a maximum number of touches.

Mickey the Mole

Mickey the Mole is digging a hole, which is no great surprise because that is what moles like to do best! Mickey is the fastest digger in the whole of 'The Underworld'. But can you beat him in a race?

Instructions

1. First, organize the children into digging teams. Each team will represent a 'digging mole' as it moves forward.

2. The children must stand in a line with their legs apart. 'Digging' is achieved by the back team member moving through the legs of the rest of the team until they become the front team member. The new back person can now move through the legs of the rest of the team until they arrive at the front, and so on.

3. Before starting, the teacher will need to show the children the finishing line for the race. When the last person in the team has crossed this line, their race will be deemed to have finished.

Focus
Cooperation, coordination
Number in group
4 or more
Equipment
None
Aim
To 'tunnel' forward as a team as quickly as possible.

Extension: Extending the length of the course or increasing the size of the teams will increase the difficulty.

43 Team-building Activities for Key Stage 1
© Gavin Middlewood and Andrew Debenham

Hoops of health

Easy

Life as a pirate is hard. Not only do you have to cope with the raging winds, the stormy seas and the continuous battles with enemy ships, you also have to look out for precious gifts to take back to your king, the mighty Rondo. Last time, you brought him back a special drink from your travels that you pretended was an exotic wine. However, you know that it was actually something else! Ssssh! This time you need to bring him back a different item. You have found some interesting hoops on the island. If you bring them back to Rondo, you plan to tell him that they are magic hoops that will restore his good health. You will tell him that if he skips through them one hundred times a day for thirty days, then his already good looks will become even more magnificent! But first, you will need to get the hoops onto your ship.

Focus
Cooperation, coordination
Number in group
2
Equipment
Hoops
Small cones/markers
PE mat
Aim
To roll the hoop in and out of the cones and finally, onto the mat.

Instructions

1. The small cones should be laid out in lines across the island (playing area). A mat should be placed at one end to represent the ship.

2. Give each pair a hoop. Their job is to work together to roll the hoop in and out of the trees (cones) along the island. Their hoop should remain upright and in contact with the ground at all times. If the hoop falls or is lifted from the ground, then the pair should return to the start.

3. When each pair arrives at the ship (mat), they will need to give it one more gentle push so that it lands on the ship. They cannot get on board until the hoop has come to rest.

Extension: Timed races between the pirates makes this a competitive challenge!

The Great Wazzoo

Wazzoo is King of the monkeys and he is hungry. Wazzoo is a good king, Wazzoo is a powerful king, but when he is hungry, Wazzoo can become a very angry king! Your little group of monkeys must go out into the jungle and collect his favourite foods. You will then need to travel across 'The Bridge of Howlers' to give him his mango, peanuts and 'sugar vine'. If you feed him perfect food then you will make him very happy. BUT...do not dare to bruise, bite or drop anything...or else!

Instructions

1. Divide the class into groups of three. Allocate a bridge (bench) to each group. Then show them the mangoes, sugar vine and peanuts (quoits, ropes and balls).

2. Tell the children that they must each take one of each food item across the bridge to the Monkey King. They must go over the bridge one at a time as it isn't strong enough for two monkeys.

3. They must adhere to the following carrying rules:

   (i) When travelling across the bridge, monkeys must hold on to the bridge with both hands and feet to keep them safe.

   (ii) Monkeys cannot hold the food in their hands or teeth as this will damage it.

Focus
Problem-solving, communication, balance
Number in group
3
Equipment
PE benches
Quoits
Skipping ropes
Small balls
Aim
To transport each individual piece of equipment across the bench without holding it or dropping it.

(iii) If any food is dropped, it will be damaged and it must be left. The monkey who dropped it needs to go back to the beginning and get a fresh piece of food.

4. Repeat the activity with the children swapping which food items they carry across the bridge.

Extension: King Wazzoo is very impatient. Each child needs to transport all three items at the same time.

The fragile dinosaur eggs

Easy

You all know how lovely baby Trufflits are! Those cuddly little blue and green dinosaurs have such lovely shiny big black eyes, don't they? You have found a nest of Trufflit eggs and sadly their mum and dad have been killed by hunters. You need to get the eggs back to your base quickly so that you can keep them warm and safe. The eggs are heavy but also very, very fragile. It will take two of you to carry each egg out of the nest and to safety. For every egg that you rescue, a wonderful baby Trufflit will be born!

Focus
Communication, balance
Number in group
2
Equipment
Large balls
Hoops
Aim
To work as a co-ordinated pair, to transport each ball along the course without dropping it.

Instructions

1. You will need to construct a course consisting of a line of holes (hoops), with a collection of Trufflit eggs (large balls) at the starting end.

2. Divide the children into pairs and get them to stand at the start of the course.

3. Explain to the children that they may only move the eggs to the other end of the course using the special carrying technique. This involves standing opposite each other and pressing against either side of the ball with their palms applying equal pressure. Fingers should be facing upwards.

4. Pairs press an egg into position and then move along the course. When they come to a hole, they must carry the egg over the top of it whilst walking either side themselves. Different size hoops will force them to move closer and further apart as they travel.

Extension: The addition of a rope bridge (bench) along which the children must travel will increase the range of movements and difficulty.

43 Team-building Activities for Key Stage 1
© Gavin Middlewood and Andrew Debenham

Sink the ship

You and your fellow pirates are sailing the Seven Seas on your trusty ship, 'The Golden Parrot'. Pirate Pete has just acquired some new cannonballs and is keen to use them in battle against the enemy ship. In the distance you see your enemy, 'The Black Rat'. In the past you have not done very well in battles against this ship. Will you be able to beat 'The Black Rat' with the help of your new cannonballs?

Focus
Coordination, cooperation
Number in group
2-4
Equipment
Beanbags
Hoops
Skipping ropes
Aim
To land ten bean bags in a designated hoop.

Instructions

1. Show the pirates (children) where the 'The Black Rat' (hoop) is.

2. Each team must decide the order in which they will throw their cannonballs (beanbags), as only one person may throw these at a time.

3. The team needs to make a line onboard their ship, 'The Golden Parrot' (marked with a skipping rope). The team must pass the first cannonball along the line until it reaches the front pirate. The front pirate can then aim their cannonball into 'The Black Rat' (hoop).

4. If the cannonball misses 'The Black Rat', the person who threw it should run and pick up the cannonball, and then rejoin their group at the back of the line. If they 'score', then they must collect a new cannonball before rejoining the line.

5. The activity is complete when ten cannonballs have sunk 'The Black Rat'.

Extensions: This activity can be made harder by extending the distance between 'The Golden Parrot' and 'The Black Rat'. Asking each child to use their 'wrong' hand to throw also provides an extra challenge.

---

43 Team-building Activities for Key Stage 1
© Gavin Middlewood and Andrew Debenham

The magic circle

Zed the Witch has stolen The Wizard Zalbo's talking owl and is keeping him locked away in a small dark prison! The wizard needs the help of you and your friends to open the magically locked trapdoor. The wizard tells you that you, his friends and helpers ARE the key! You will need to form a magic circle around the door and then follow the wizard's instructions very, very carefully! If you can do this then the spell will be broken and the owl will be freed!

Instructions

1. For this activity you are the Wizard. Organize the children into groups around the mats. The groups should be of a size that, when they hold hands, they are just able to walk around the trapdoor (mat) without touching it.

2. Tell the children they need to join hands and on no account let go, or this will result in the failure of the 'release spell'.

3. The wizard (teacher) should now relay a series of instructions. Here are some examples:

   (i) Move clockwise until I say stop!

   (ii) Move anti-clockwise until I tell you to stop!

Focus
Cooperation, communication
Number in group
4-8
Equipment
PE mats
Aim
To follow the instructions carefully, whilst keeping hold of each other's hands and without stepping onto the mat.

43 Team-building Activities for Key Stage 1
© Gavin Middlewood and Andrew Debenham

(iii) All balance on your right leg while I count to ten.

(iv) All balance on your left leg while I count to ten.

(v) Name a child to lean over the trapdoor!

4. When the wizard is happy that the children have completed the spell then the owl is free and the activity is complete.

Extension: Larger group sizes around two mats positioned together will increase the difficulty of the cooperation required.

Battle of the Bouncers

It is the year 2108 and humans live alongside robots on Earth. Your best robot friends, Buddytron and Happytron, have challenged you and your best human friend to a ball bouncing competition. You and your friend need to take turns to bounce a ball inside a hoop, using just one hand. However, you must alternate who hits the ball with every bounce. You must do this continuously, without stopping or catching the ball. Buddytron and Happytron are very proud of their record. They have scored nine. Can you beat their score?

Focus
Coordination, cooperation
Number in group
4-30 players, divided into teams of 2-5
Equipment
Large balls
Hoops
Aim
To bounce the ball continuously inside the hoop, with each partner taking turns between every bounce.

Instructions

1. Let the children practise bouncing their ball individually in the playing area. They should get used to the bounce of the ball and the space that they have.

2. Pairs must now work together to achieve consecutive bounces in which they take turns after every bounce. The children's first target can be ten.

3. Once the target is achieved, the pairs must now attempt to make their best possible score in setting a new record.

Extensions: Challenge the children to reach their target using their 'weaker' hand. Alternatively, using alternate hands will require some greater thought and concentration.

Use your heads!

The king of all of Gazaban, King Rondo, has a son called Prince Larry. Prince Larry loves to play with toys. Unfortunately, there are not many toys to play with in Gazaban. Especially not since the wicked witch Zed destroyed them all with a nasty spell of hers. Rondo has ordered you to bring him some toys for Prince Larry to play with. In your bag you have a quoit, a beanbag and a tennis ball. Prince Larry should have fun with them! The only problem is that you need to cross the moat that surrounds King Rondo's castle without the items getting wet. Larry doesn't like wet toys, you see. What are you going to do? Use your head!

Focus
Balance, problem-solving
Number in group
2
Equipment
Quoits
Tennis balls
Beanbags
Aim
To transport the three items using only your head.

Instructions

1. Give each pair two quoits, two beanbags and two tennis balls.

2. Tell the children that they will need to transport the items across the moat (marked playing area) and they can only use their heads to do so. The only time that they may use their hands is in front of the moat so that they can put the items on their heads. Give the pupils planning time so that they can discuss tactics.

3. Once the pupils are happy with their plans, the task can begin. If items are dropped, they automatically become wet and unfit for Prince Larry. Therefore, the children must return to the start and try again.

Hint: Placing the tennis ball on top of the beanbag, and the beanbag inside the quoit often proves a useful strategy.

Extension: You can extend this task by varying the range of items.

Crystal balls

You are in the magical land of Gazaban. Your mission is to take a magical crystal ball across the shimmery silver fields to Wizard Zalbo. As usual though, wicked Witch Zed has tried to stop you! She has cast a spell which means that you cannot move. However, if you are in possession of the magical crystal ball, its powers will allow the person holding it to move! All of the group needs to be careful crossing the field. Should the crystal be dropped, its powers will be lost forever.

Instructions

1. Sort the children into groups and give them some time to plan how they will cross the shimmering silver fields (playing area).

2. The groups must attempt to cross the fields. As soon as they set foot on the fields their feet should remain frozen until they are in the possession of the crystal. If the crystal is dropped, the team should return to the start.

Focus
Problem-solving, cooperation
Number in group
3-5
Equipment
Tennis balls
Aim
To transport the whole group across the playing area with only the person holding the ball being allowed to move.

Hint: The children could form a line. The crystal can then be passed from the front to the back of the line. Then, the back person will need to run to the front with the crystal and the process can be repeated.

Extension: This activity can be repeated in the format of a race with obstacles introduced such as hurdles (fences) or benches (high bridges).

Feed the crabs

You are a crab and your name is Carl. Carl the Crab! You live with your brother, Clint, who happens to be a crab too. The two of you have lots of fun together in your rock pool. You splash around in the water and chase lobsters every day. However, like most brothers, you have your arguments from time to time. Your mother, Catrina Crab, wants you to practise sharing your food with one another. You mustn't use your claws; otherwise the food will get crushed. Also, if you drop it, those nasty lobsters will take it for themselves. Can you pass your food to one another?

Focus
Coordination, problem-solving, balance
Number in group
2
Equipment
Beanbags or quoits
Aim
To pass the beanbag to each other without using hands, or it touching the floor.

Instructions

1. The children should practise making a crab shape. This is done by placing both of their hands and feet on the floor, with their chest facing upwards. Once the children have made a crab shape they can practise moving around the rock pool (playing area).

2. Divide the crabs (pupils) into pairs and give each pair a piece of food (beanbag).

3. The food should be balanced on one of the crab's chests. This crab should then work with their partner to transfer the food to their partner's chest, without touching it with their claw (hand) or the food touching the floor.

4. Once this has been achieved the pair should attempt to transfer it back again. How many times can they successfully transfer the food without dropping it?

Extension: Turn the activity into a race in which crabs have to move over a set distance before passing the food to their partner.

Island capture

Medium

King Rondo has a dream. He wants his kingdom to grow to the size of the neighbouring country, the U.S.I. (United States of Igara). Rondo sets you and your fellow pirates on board 'The Golden Parrot' the task of capturing as many islands as possible for his kingdom. However, some of the islands in the ocean are being controlled by other pirates from other countries. Can you capture the remaining islands for your king? As you may already know, he is an impatient man, so get it done … fast!

Instructions

1. Place the sequencing spots/cones over the ocean (playing area) – an equal number of each colour. Cones of the same colour should be spread apart from each other.

2. Divide the pirates (children) into pairs. Each pair should begin on an island (cone) of their choice. No two pairs can start on the same island.

3. Tell the pairs that they will need to work together to capture all of the islands which are the same colour as their starting island. They must plan a route together that will enable them to visit all the islands of their colour, as quickly as possible. They should remember this route, as once they have visited all the islands they need to do the same route in reverse order to succeed in their mission. At each island (cone) they come to, both children must bend down and touch it with one hand. (They should not pick the cones up.)

Focus
Agility, problem-solving
Number in group
2
Equipment
20-30 coloured sequencing spots or small cones/markers of at least 4 different colours
Aim
For pairs to visit all of the sequencing spots of their colour as quickly as possible.

43 Team-building Activities for Key Stage 1
© Gavin Middlewood and Andrew Debenham

4. After planning time, give the children two minutes (or longer, depending on the size of the ocean) to capture as many islands as possible for King Rondo. They must remember to keep track of their score.

5. When this has been completed, the children should move to a different coloured island. The task is repeated. Can the pair beat their record?

Extension: Larger oceans will require greater agility and stamina from the pirates.

The fantastic photo competition

You and your team have entered 'The Fantastic Portrait Photograph Competition'. The first prize is a holiday for you and your friends to the place that you went to in your dreams last night! The photographer, Mr. Snappit, has been taking photos for the past 50 years and he knows what makes a winning photograph. When he gives you an instruction, make sure that you do it as well as you can so that you stand a chance of winning that fantastic, magical prize!

Focus
Problem-solving, balance
Number in group
3-7 (mixed sex)
Equipment
PE benches
Aim
For team members to arrange themselves on the bench according to instructions.

Instructions

1. The teacher, in the role of Mr. Snappit, asks the children to stand on the bench in any order for the first photograph. Once they have had their photo taken, Mr. Snappit informs them that he is not happy with the picture and that he would like to take some others. Children should reorganize themselves to comply with the following instructions:

   (i)   Line up shortest to tallest

   (ii) Place a girl/boy at either end

   (iii) Group all of the boys/girls together

   (iv) Line up the lightest hair to the darkest hair

   (v)   Line up the shortest hair to the longest hair

   (vi) Line up the shortest name to the longest name.

Extension: Children can be instructed that as they change positions, their feet are not allowed to touch the floor.

Transporters

A robot that transforms into a motorbike! Another robot that changes into a speedboat! A third that becomes a racing car. This is the future, but the future is now! You have ordered a special delivery and 'The Transporters' are on their way, but can you guess which one will be arriving at your door?

Instructions

1. Allocate one member of each group to be the 'guesser'. The remainder of the group will be the transporters.

2. The transporter picks up a vehicle card and then picks up a special delivery (bean bag). They must now mime their vehicle whilst transporting the special delivery. The bean bag must not be held in their hands, but balanced upon their bodies.

3. When the 'guesser' guesses correctly, the transporter chooses a new card, and the activity is repeated. Each time that the guesser correctly identifies the vehicle, they are allowed to keep the special delivery being carried by that particular transporter!

Focus
Balance, non-verbal communication
Number in group
2-3
Equipment
Bean bags
Transport cards (Resource Sheet on page 59)
Aim
To mime a vehicle in such a way that a team member will be able to guess it correctly.

Extension: Instead of miming, the transporter must create the shape of their transport vehicle (this works best with pairs of transporters working together).

King Rondo's dinner

King Rondo is hungry and wants his dinner served. He is so important that he expects his servants to bring dinner to him, from the kitchen to his table. He has a huge appetite so it usually requires several of his staff to carry his dinner as it weighs so much. King Rondo wants his dinner served quickly, as he is an impatient man, and we don't want to upset the King!

Instructions

1. Each group should choose one member to become King Rondo. It will be the job of the servants (the other pupils) to serve him.

2. All of the equipment should be stationed at one end of the playing area representing the kitchen. All of the King Rondos should position themselves at the other end and wait to be served.

3. The servants should then serve the food (the equipment) on their plates (bats) to King Rondo. Both servants must hold the plates at all times and must only touch the food when putting it on the plate. If any of the food is dropped at any time during service then the servants must return to the kitchen and start again. The King won't eat dirty food! Service should be completed in three stages:

   (i)   Starter of spaghetti. The skipping rope should be balanced on the plate and taken to King Rondo.

   (ii)   Main course of pie and beans (one ball and one beanbag).

   (iii)   Dessert of ice-cream (one ball)

Focus
Cooperation, coordination, agility
Number in group
3
Equipment
Bats
Balls
Skipping ropes
Bean bags
Aim
To transport the items from one end of the playing area to the other in pairs using the bats provided.

43 **Team-building Activities for Key Stage 1**
© Gavin Middlewood and Andrew Debenham

4. When this has been completed the task should be repeated with a different member of the group becoming King Rondo.

Extension: The dinner hall is crowded. The servants need to weave their way towards Rondo around and over a variety of benches and through a number of cones.

Twins in trouble

It is the age of Robin Hood and times are hard in your small village. The crops have failed and you have no food. Fortunately, Robin Hood has given you some gold and you have travelled to the city of Nottingham to buy bread! Unfortunately, the evil Sheriff of Nottingham has captured you and taken the gold away! To make things worse he has chained you and your twin together so that you will find it very hard to run away! However, if you can climb across the bridge and through the trees you may be able to get back to the safety of Sherwood Forest.

Focus
Cooperation, communication
Number in group
2
Equipment
Hoops
PE benches
Cones/markers
Aim
To move in pairs though an obstacle course whilst staying connected by a hoop.

Instructions

1. Create an escape route from Nottingham including the bridge (bench) and the trees (cones). Divide the children into pairs of twins and line them up at the start.

2. Tell the pairs that they are chained together (with a hoop). They must travel the course whilst both remaining chained together. They must NOT use their hands to hold the hoop nor become disconnected whilst navigating the course. If they should do so, then they must start again. The hoop must not touch the floor throughout the activity.

3. Place the hoop over the two children in a position suggested by them. Through teamwork, they must create the tension that will support the hoop as they travel.

Extension: Adding additional bridges (benches) that the pairs must travel over will make this activity much harder.

43 Team-building Activities for Key Stage 1
© Gavin Middlewood and Andrew Debenham

Beware of the prickle

Deep in the jungles of Selva, lives a tiny, endangered animal called the Bandook. A Bandook looks very much like a hedgehog except it is brightly coloured. It is different from a hedgehog in one other very important way. Every single one of its spikes holds a deadly poison! You have been exploring the jungle looking for Bandooks. When you find the Bandooks, you need to guide them into the carrying case before taking them back to the Nature Reserve. They may be poisonous, but they are also very jumpy, so as you move them you must be extremely careful and quiet. If you frighten them they might run away, or worse still, jump up into your arms!

Focus
Communication, coordination
Number in group
2
Equipment
Small balls
Small bats
Large hoops
PE benches
Aim
To direct the balls up, along and off the bench and into a hoop using the bats provided.

Instructions

1. Place a carrying case (hoop) at the far end of the bridge (bench).

2. Pairs of children may now attempt to gently lift a Bandook (small ball) up and onto the bridge using their special gloves (small bats). Children will need to work carefully together in order to direct the Bandook forwards using the small bats whilst not allowing the Bandook to fall from the bridge. They will also need to stop the ball at the end of the bridge in order to carefully deposit it into the carrying case below.

3. If a Bandook falls from the bridge, it will escape and you will need to start again!

Extension: Two benches placed at right angles to each other will provide a challenge for specialist Bandook hunters.

Pirate treasure

You are a pirate and with your friends you sail the Seven Seas in your ship called 'The Golden Parrot'! Today you have fought a long battle with another band of pirates who sail in their ship called 'The Black Rat!' One of your cannonballs has just gone straight through their ship and out the other side! 'The Black Rat' is sinking but it is full of treasure chests full of gold and silver. These are filling up with water fast! It won't be long before they sink to the bottom of the ocean and the treasure will be lost FOREVER!

The chests are heavy so you will need to work with a partner to bring them back aboard 'The Golden Parrot'. You will need your arms and legs to swim, so can you balance the treasure chests between your chests?

Focus
Cooperation, coordination
Number in group
2
Equipment
Large balls
Skipping ropes or markers to define play areas
Aim
To transport the balls across the playing area without dropping them, or using hands.

Instructions

1. Use skipping ropes or markets to show where the two ships are situated.

2. Divide the children into pairs.

3. Each pair will need to place the ball between their chests and travel back to 'The Golden Parrot' without the ball dropping. Children must not touch the ball with their hands whilst travelling, as they will need to make swimming motions with their arms!

4. If they drop their chest they must return to 'The Black Rat' and start again.

Extension: This activity can be completed within a time limit. Children can work in a group of three to transport two chests at once.

43 Team-building Activities for Key Stage 1
© Gavin Middlewood and Andrew Debenham

Float away

Welcome to the future! Professor Levitas has just invented the ultimate toy ... a flying skateboard. You can buy floating bands and lots of other small floating things from shops but the skateboard is the biggest floating toy so far! You and your friends have climbed to the top of a very tall building to play in the rooftop garden. Then disaster strikes, one of your friends crashes the flying skateboard on the next-door skyscraper! Your friend is as stuck as a blackbird baked in a pie! Luckily, you have a collection of floating bands, and four of them could be enough to carry a small person through the air, and back to safety!

Focus
Problem-solving, coordination
Number in group
2
Equipment
Quoits
Hoops
Aim
To throw the quoits in such a way so that they are 'caught' on the limbs of their partner.

Instructions

1. Two hoops must be positioned to represent the skyscrapers. The rescue person must stand on one skyscraper and the crash victim on the other. The rescue person will need a supply of floating bands (quoits) nearby.

2. The teacher tells the crash victim that to fly to safety he must catch a band for each arm and leg. There are 2 additional rules: Each band must be caught with the appropriate limb! Any band hitting the floor will be broken, and therefore cannot be used.

3. The rescue person must attempt to throw the quoits so that they land on the limbs of their partner.

4. After trying this activity, the children should swap roles.

Hint: The crash victim may find it easier to catch the bands if they lie down!

Extension: The skyscrapers can be moved further apart to increase difficulty.

The ring robbers

Do you know what a goblin is? Goblins are mischievous creatures. Goblins love hunting for treasure and that is why you and your goblin friends are now in a dragon's cave trying to steal his precious gold and diamond rings. Some of your goblin friends are stuck on the other side of a deep valley. Will you be able to silently steal the rings and pass them across this deep gap in the ground without waking up the dragon? If you make a noise it could be roast goblin on the menu tonight!

Focus
Coordination, problem-solving
Number in group
3-4
Equipment
Quoits
Skipping ropes
Aim
To transfer the quoits from one part of the group to the other across the gap, without dropping them.

Instructions

1. Use skipping ropes to mark out where the valley is. This area should be no wider than the length of the skipping ropes available.

2. A dragon's treasure pile of rings (quoits) and ropes should be placed on one side of the ravine.

3. Put the children into groups of 3 or 4 and then split each group so that the two parts of the group are opposite, facing each other across the gap.

4. The children on the side with the equipment now need to sneak to the dragon's treasure pile and take the rings one at a time. They now have to work out how to transport them to their team-mates across the ravine quietly without dropping them and waking the dragon. This precious treasure must not be thrown as this will damage it.

Extensions: To add a competitive edge, the different coloured quoits could represent different values. Using larger PE hoops, instead of quoits, will increase the chances of making a noise!

43 Team-building Activities for Key Stage 1
© Gavin Middlewood and Andrew Debenham

Jewels of the Nile

Medium

You and your friends are a band of explorers searching for gold and diamonds in Egypt. As you walk alongside the River Nile you notice something shining brightly in a deep hole beside the river. You clamber down the hole and, to your amazement there lie four precious diamonds in front of you! Unfortunately you have no pockets to put the diamonds in and you'll need both of your hands to climb out of the hole. Can you throw them carefully out of the hole for your friends to catch?

Focus
Cooperation, coordination
Number in group
3
Equipment
Hoops
Beanbags
Aim
To throw the beanbags through the hoop and catch them on the other side.

Instructions

1. In each group, one child should be chosen to be the 'diamond finder'. Their job will be to throw the diamonds (beanbags) through the hole in the ground (hoop).

2. A second child must hold the hoop above their head whilst the third child catches the diamonds after they have travelled through the hoop.

3. Give the 'diamond finder' four diamonds. They must attempt to throw the diamonds one by one through the hoop. This should be held at least one metre away from the 'diamond finder'. Each time the diamond is caught by the 'catcher' the team scores one point.

4. After the four diamonds have been thrown, the children swap roles so that the 'diamond finder' holds the hoop, the hoop holder becomes the catcher and the catcher is now the 'diamond finder'

5. After four more throws, the children swap roles to take up their last position. The team then has a score out of twelve.

Extension: Using tennis balls will test the catching skills of the children further.

Rocking in the swamp

You and your band of brave explorers are travelling deep into the Evergreen Swamps. This watery land is beautiful, but deadly! You have come to a particularly dangerous bit! The good news is that there is a path through the middle and your friends have a map. The bad news is that if you step into the swamp by mistake then you may sink, disappear and never be seen again. Thank goodness you have your lucky rock to throw and check that the ground is solid enough to stand on.

Focus
Communication, coordination
Number in group
2-3
Equipment
Bean bags
Colour sequence cards (Resource sheet on page 60)
Coloured hoops: yellow, red, blue, green
Aim
To follow a designated route whilst throwing a beanbag into the upcoming hoop.

Instructions

1. Construct the swamp by laying down a number of coloured hoops. These may be touching each other or have a small space in between.

2. Divide the children into groups of 2-3. Each group should nominate someone to be the explorer. The explorer needs to find a path through the swamp (the hoops). In order to move into a hoop safely, they will need to throw their rock into it. This ensures that the ground is safe.

3. The child(ren) with a map (colour sequence card) will shout out the first colour on their list. It is up to the explorer to throw their rock into a hoop of that colour. If they are successful then they can move to that hoop. Then the second colour is read out, and so on. If the throw misses the designated hoop, then the explorer must return to the start!

Hint: Make sure that the required jump is not too great as the hoops can slide easily along wooden floors.

Extensions: Increasing the space in between the hoops demands greater aiming and throwing ability. A number of groups can explore the swamp simultaneously.

© Gavin Middlewood and Andrew Debenham

The finding spell

Princess Wilma has gone missing. The King has sent people to search the land far and wide but still there is no sign of her. Finally he has asked the Wizard Zalbo for help. The wizard has sent you to see 'The 3 Witches' to ask them for a special 'Finding Spell'. The witches live high in a cave, across a bridge above the city. In order to get there you must travel for 3 days and 3 nights. When you arrive, the witches agree to give you the spell. The problem is that no one is allowed to write in the witches' cave in case they steal other spells by copying them out! You must cross the bridge one at a time and try to remember every word as a team.

Focus
Communication
Number in group
3-6
Equipment
Writing materials
Spell cards (Resource sheet on page 61)
Aim
To use memory to correctly relay a long message to the rest of the team as quickly as possible.

Instructions

1. Each team needs to decide who will be the scribe – the person who writes down the spell. This player will move to the opposite side of the playing area and pick up the writing materials.

2. Upon the teacher's signal, the rest of the group can look at their collection of words or spells. Start with just one spell and build up.

3. This group must now decide how to relay this message to the scribe in the most efficient manner. They may only cross the playing area one at a time.

4. As each player arrives with their part of the message, the scribe writes it down.

5. When the scribe is confident that he has the complete spell, he takes this answer to the teacher to discover if this is correct. If read out correctly, then the princess can now be found!

Extensions: The sentences can be made more complex and the playing area extended. The difficulty of the words given should depend upon the literacy skills of the children. Also, the wizard (you) may decide that all words must be spelt correctly.

The snowy mountain

You are in a team of explorers climbing one of the highest mountains in the world. However, it is getting icy at the top and your feet are starting to slip. Luckily, you have some special 'grippers' in your rucksack that will stop you slipping on this very important part of the journey. You will need to pass these to the front without letting go of the rope and use them to build a path to the top of the mountain.

Instructions

1. Each group will need to form a line and hold onto the rope while standing on their bench. This represents the mountain. In front of each bench should be at least 3 metres of ice field (playing area) that the children need to cross.

2. Each team should be given 5 grippers (quoits) to put at the back of their bench.

3. The member at the back of the line must feed the (skipping) rope through the grippers (quoits). The grippers should then be manoeuvred to the front of the line through careful 'wiggles' of the rope. Team members must have at least one hand on the rope, otherwise they will fall from the mountain. The grippers can only be passed one at a time along the rope and must not be touched.

4. The front person must then use the grippers that they receive to build a path in front of them. As the path is built, the team must balance upon these as well as hold the rope with both hands.

5. As soon as every member has passed across the ice field, the task is complete.

Focus
Cooperation, balance
Number in group
3-6
Equipment
Quoits
Skipping ropes
PE benches
Aim
To pass the grippers (quoits) along the rope and use them to build a path across the ice (playing area).

Extension: Creating a larger ice field will require improved balance and skill from the pupils.

43 Team-building Activities for Key Stage 1
© Gavin Middlewood and Andrew Debenham

Journey to the centre of the Earth

Medium

WOW! Rubies, emeralds, sapphires and diamonds ... just lying around on the ground! Look at them all, sparkling in the dust! You wish that you could just walk over and pick them up, don't you? Things are never that easy. Only those special little digging machines can dig a hole to the middle of the earth to collect them. So, it's time to climb into your diggers and to work hard until your buckets are full of fantastic, colourful treasure!

Focus
Coordination, problem solving
Number in group
2-5
Equipment
Hoops
Red, blue, green and yellow bean bags
Aim
To transport a beanbag of each colour back into the hoop in the designated manner.

Instructions

1. Sort the children into groups of miners and give each group a basket (hoop). The rubies, sapphires, emeralds and diamonds (beanbags) need to be scattered around the playing area.

2. Tell the miners that they must collect one of each of the jewels and return them to their bucket (hoop) following these movement rules:

   (i) They must only travel in the 'crab' (belly to the ceiling) posture.

   (ii) Jewels must be picked up by the machine's claws (feet). No hands may be used.

   (iii) Miners cannot move along when they have a beanbag in their feet. They can however rotate on their bottoms and then pass the beanbag on to a team member.

3. The task is completed when the team has transported one of each of the colours back into their hoop.

Extension: The requirement can be raised to two beanbags of each colour. The task can be timed in a race format. Balls can be used to represent the jewels.

Fishing for dinner

You are sailors on the pirate ship 'The Golden Parrot'. Pirate Pete has dropped you off on a deserted island to search for food such as pineapples, bananas and maize. He has sailed away and will pick you and the food up in a week's time! There is a small problem ... there has been a terrible forest fire on the island and there is no food to be found. You are very hungry. You can see some delicious looking fish in the deep, dangerous waters but how will you catch them without rods or nets?

Focus
Cooperation, problem-solving
Number in group
2-3
Equipment
Hoops
Skipping ropes
Bean bags
Aim
To retrieve the fish (beanbags) using the equipment provided.

Instructions

1. Identify the shoreline using skipping ropes and tell the children that they cannot step beyond this line into the sea.

2. The fish should be placed in the sea at varying distances. Some should be within hoop range, some the distance of one skipping rope and some yet further.

3. Divide the children into groups and tell them that they are to catch the fish using the vines (ropes) and bamboo hoops (hoops) constructed from what is left of the forest!

Extensions: A more competitive environment could be developed by grouping the fish in colours. The colour of fish that are furthest away could be worth more because they are harder to catch.

43 Team-building Activities for Key Stage 1
© Gavin Middlewood and Andrew Debenham

Light up the night!

How does an aeroplane know where to land at night when there is no moon? The pilot follows the landing lights that show him exactly where to go. At Gazaban Airport, the lights have been broken and someone needs to go out into the dark to fix them! The trouble is that it is SO dark that you cannot see your hand in front of your face! You will need the computer operators back at base to tell you what to do and when you have finished the job. You will need to hurry. There is already one plane circling above, wanting to land, and more are expected soon.

Focus
Communication, problem-solving
Number in group
2-3
Equipment
Beanbags
Hoops
Blindfolds
Aim
To organize the beanbags into hoops of the same colour whilst blindfolded.

Instructions

1. Arrange 3 hoops of different colours and place 2 beanbags of the same colour inside each hoop.

2. Explain to the children that this is what the landing lights look like when they are working properly.

3. Sort the children into groups and identify one member in each group to be the mechanic working in the dark. This member must stand next to the hoops and be blindfolded.

4. Now change the beanbags around so that the colours are no longer co-ordinated. Inform the group that the lights are now broken and there is a plane coming in to land. It is their job to fix them in the quickest time that they can.

5. Explain that only the mechanic in the dark can fix the lights as the rest of the ground crew must stay back at base and watch the computers to tell him how he is doing, and to help the mechanic put the beanbags into the correct hoops.

Extensions: More beanbags will complicate the task. Words could be limited to 'yes', 'no', 'right' and 'left'.

Monsters of the Universe

The year is 2508. Buses, trains and even aeroplanes are things of the past. Most people now travel in spaceships — not from town to town anymore, but from planet to planet. It's only a two minute flight in your 'Turbo Blaster' spaceship to get a loaf of bread from Venus! Except you don't want bread anymore. Or any food in fact! Why not? Because you are aliens! Aliens made up from many arms and many legs. Special aliens who can change shape as you roam the Solar System. Every planet has its preferred body shape, and you can change into them all!

Focus
Communication, problem-solving, balance
Number in group
2
Equipment
None
Aim
To work with a partner to complete the body shapes for each planet.

Instructions

1. Divide the pupils into pairs. Tell them that they will need to work together to complete the body shapes when they arrive at each planet. Each shape should be held for ten seconds.

   (i)   **Mercury:** Pairs need to ensure that one pupil's elbow touches their partner's knee.

   (ii) **Venus:** One foot in contact with the back of the second child.

   (iii) **Earth:** Both children stand up normally, but still.

   (iv) **Mars:** Both children stand on one leg each. They may support each other if this helps.

   (v)   **Jupiter:** One child can have feet only on the floor. Their partner can have their hands only on the floor. The children must remain in contact with each other.

   (vi) **Saturn:** The children must both lie down and together, make a circle shape to represent a ring.

   (vii) **Uranus:** A shoulder from one pupil should be held against the back of another.

   (viii)**Neptune:** Both children must balance only on their knees. They should support each other.

   (ix) **Pluto:** Both children may only balance on their shoulders/upper backs. They should, again, support their partner.

Extension: The children should attempt to remember some of the shapes for each planet. The teacher calls out a random planet and the children respond with the appropriate shape.

Alien invasion

We are in the future, 1000 years on from now and aliens have arrived from planet Neptune. Unfortunately for the human race, they have begun to take over planet Earth. These aliens are very dangerous so it is important for humans to stay out of their way. However, there is bad news ... the aliens are hungry!

Instructions

1. Choose two pairs of pupils to become aliens. The four-legged aliens are formed by two children each holding onto the same quoit. Their job will be to 'tag' as many humans as possible within the allotted time.

2. The rest of the group now become humans. Their job will be to avoid any contact with the aliens. Humans are only allowed to walk in this activity.

3. The aliens now have one minute (or however long you decide) to 'tag' as many humans as possible. Each half of the alien must not let go of the quoit at any time, otherwise the alien automatically melts to dust and is out of the game. Each time a human is 'tagged' they should visit the hospital and perform ten star jumps to shake off the alien's germs. The hospital (mat) is situated next to the designated playing area.

4. When the allotted time has elapsed, the aliens' scores should be given to the teacher (ie how many humans they have managed to tag). New aliens can then be chosen and the game starts again.

Focus
Communication, cooperation
Number in group
2-4 (aliens), remainder of class (humans)
Equipment
Quoits
PE mat
Aim
Aliens: To catch as many humans as they can in the allotted time.

Humans: To avoid the aliens for as long as possible.

Extension: Aliens made up of three or four children will need greater cooperation skills.

The slippery snake

You and your friends are on a journey across Australia. However, as you pass the famous River Darling, your eyes meet a deadly snake. Luckily, you have had some advice in dealing with these poisonous creatures. 'Take it across the River Darling!' cries Sarah, the snake expert. 'Make sure that you use those special snake gloves. But whatever you do, don't drop it!'

Instructions

1. Place a snake (skipping rope) in front of each pair of children. The groups should also be given two snake gloves (quoits) that they will use to pick the snake up.

2. Once they have picked up the snake, pairs should attempt to carry it across the river (playing area) using the snake gloves provided. The snake must not touch any part of the children's body/clothes at any time. If the snake is dropped, the pupils must return to the start and try again.

3. After the children have successfully crossed the river they should put the snake down carefully using their gloves. The task is now complete.

Focus
Problem-solving, coordination
Number in group
2
Equipment
Quoits
Skipping ropes
Aim
To transport the skipping rope from one end of the playing area to the other using the quoits.

Extension: Snakes everywhere! How many snakes can the pairs successfully transfer in a set time period?

The mighty Magnetron

In the future much of the world is run by robots: robots in factories, robot cleaners, robot teachers and many more. The man who makes the robots is called Magnetron. To make the robots he needs to collect something called 'Glox', which is a metal found at the very centre of the Earth. Magnetron has sent you, his mining robots to dig for more 'Glox'. If you work together then you will be able to collect enough, but watch out, 'Glox' is very magnetic and you are made of metal!

Focus
Teamwork, balance
Number in group
4-8
Equipment
Quoits
PE benches
Aim
To move along a bench in order to collect quoits which are then used to link members of the team to each other.

Instructions

1. Line up the group of children at one end of the mineshaft (bench). At the opposite end there must be lumps of Glox (quoits), one for each person in the group.

2. The first mining robot must cross the bench and collect a lump of Glox. He then returns to the rest of the group holding the lump of Glox magnetized to his hand! As soon as the next in line takes hold of the quoit they will be deemed 'stuck'. The pair now travel back and pick up a second quoit. They will return to the group where a third robot will join on the growing line.

3. The children must move backwards and forwards along the bench until all of the Glox is collected. They may need to turn at points but they must remain on the bench at all times.

4. This activity should then repeated with the group working in reverse order to the first time.

Extension: The activity can be timed and, if children become unattached or step from the bench, this can incur a time penalty.

Pain in Spain

Your name is Pirate Pete and you have left your ship, 'The Golden Parrot', in search of treasure in Spain. Unfortunately, as you make your way from the beach, you come across some people who speak a different language to you. They seem fearful of your black eye patches and your funny shaped beards. 'No hablo español,' cries your partner Long Don Silver. However, this only seems to make them angrier. Luckily, Don is carrying a phrase book. Although you cannot pronounce the words, you can use the rope in your backpack to make the letters!

Focus
Cooperation, non-verbal communication
Number in group
3-4
Equipment
Skipping ropes
Spanish words (Resource sheet on page 60)
Whiteboard and pens
Aim
To communicate a Spanish word correctly using the skipping rope.

Instructions

1. One person in the group should be selected to become the Spanish native. They must stand in a viewing area away from the rest of the group. They are given a piece of slate and chalk (whiteboard and pen).

2. Give the pirates (rest of the group) the Spanish words and a skipping rope. (The number of words you give will depend on the ability of the children.) They must form the letters of the word using the skipping rope for the Spanish native to copy down on their slate.

3. When the pirates have finished they must check with the Spanish native to see if the word has been spelt correctly. If it is, they are free to continue their quest. If incorrect, they have upset the natives and are captured!

Extension: The words on the Resource Sheet increase in difficulty.

Dance of the starfish

It is a beautiful sunny morning down at the rockpool. It is also a very exciting morning as you and your starfish friends are about to perform your special dance for the King of all Starfish. It is very important that you dance in the correct way for your special visitor and you have been practising for weeks to get the dance just right. You are going to do three circles of the 'Flipping Over Dance' with your partner, but watch out for those big waves!!

Instructions

1. Children will need to find a partner with whom to practise the 'Flipping Over' movement.

2. Children need to stand back to back with their partner in the shape of a star with arms and legs apart. The movement is completed successfully by simultaneously turning through 180 degrees whilst maintaining fingertip contact with their left or right hands (depending on whether they intend to move anticlockwise or clockwise). They will now be face to face in a star shape. The next movement will return them back to back.

3. When the teacher is ready to start the dance, pairs of starfish need to form a large class circle with the hoops at their centre.

Focus
Cooperation, coordination
Number in group
Whole class in pairs
Equipment
Music (optional)
1-4 Hoops
Aim
To complete 3 or more circles of dance without any of the starfish breaking apart.

---

43 Team-building Activities for Key Stage 1
© Gavin Middlewood and Andrew Debenham

4. Children are informed that they must dance three circuits and that if they come apart in their pair then they must go to the central rock pool (hoop) to be stuck back together. This is achieved by performing 10 star jumps. They can then reclaim their place and continue the king's dance!

5. Before you start, inform the pupils that when you call out 'WAVE!', they must duck down together to stop themselves being washed away. Wait until the dance has started before calling out.

Extension: This game can be repeated with giant starfish where pairs hold hands and mirror the movements of a second pair.

The rainbow spell

The evil Witch Zed has made your magical land of Gazaban very unhappy. She has turned everything in the world black, grey and white! There are no more colours anywhere! The sea is grey, the sky is black and everyone is wearing plain, white clothes. Luckily, Wizard Zalbo has a spell to bring colour back into the world. You will need to listen very carefully to your wizard's instructions in order to bring happiness back to your planet.

Focus
Agility, communication
Number in group
4
Equipment
4 sets of different coloured hoops (at least 20 for a class of 30)
Aim
To follow the teacher's instructions by sending each member of the group to the correct coloured hoop.

Instructions

1. The wizard (you) must scatter the coloured hoops over the playing area.

2. Divide the pupils into groups of four.

3. Call out a series of instructions. These can be in the following stages:

   (i) Single colour. For example, red. On this command groups must all run to that coloured hoop as quickly as they can and ensure that everyone in their group can fit inside. This can be repeated for different colours.

   (ii) Double colour. For example, green and blue. For this, the groups will need to ensure that they split their group evenly and send half to one colour and half to the other.

   (iii) Rainbow. All groups must ensure that members are split across different coloured hoops.

   (iv) A mix of the previous three stages.

4. When the wizard is satisfied that all groups have completed the task successfully, then the spell is complete and the challenge is over.

Extension: Removing some of the hoops from the playing area will mean that more children will need to fit inside each hoop. This will necessitate improved balance and cooperation skills.

© Gavin Middlewood and Andrew Debenham

Shape up!

The land of Gazaban is often a battle between the good of Wizard Zalbo and the bad of Witch Zed. The magical spells that Zalbo casts help everyone in the battle against evil. However, recent strong winds have caused much damage to the lives of all Gazabanians. None more so, than Zalbo himself. Important pages from his spell book, 'Wizard's Guide to Wonderful Wizardry' have blown everywhere. Can you help him match up the parts to one of his spells? It is made up of numbers and coloured shapes!

Focus
Agility, communication
Number in group
2-3
Equipment
Paper and coloured pencils
8 number cards
8 simple 2D coloured shapes
Aim
To match the coloured shapes with the correct numbers on their piece of paper.

Instructions

1. Spread out the coloured shapes at one end of the playing area. Place a number card beside each shape.

2. Position the groups at the other end of the area. Give each group paper and access to coloured pencils.

3. The children need to number their paper from 1-8. Tell the children that their task is to draw the coloured shape that goes with each number on their paper. The answers lie opposite them on the other side of Gazaban (the playing area). However, the paper and pencils must remain at the end where they are standing at all times.

4. After, a short period of planning time, the task can begin. Remind the groups that the answers can be completed in any order!

5. When a group thinks that they have finished they should shout 'Spell Complete!' and their answers should then be checked.

Hints: Groups may opt to send all group members to help memorize the shape and colour. Alternatively, they may keep one person back each time and swap roles so that energy can be conserved.

Extension: Letters instead of shapes can be used. Then, using the letters found, the groups must construct the longest word possible.

Foxes and wolves

The night is nearly over and it is time for the foxes and the wolves to go home. They have been hunting all night and have a lot of meat for their families. Unfortunately, they must cross back through the same valley to get back to their homes. If the foxes and the wolves meet, then there will be another terrible battle, so they must move very carefully and very quietly to stay away from each other!

Focus
Problem-solving, communication
Number in group
2 teams of 4, 5 or 6
Equipment
9 hoops
Aim
To cross to the opposite side of the playing area without sharing a hoop with a member of the opposite team.

Instructions

1. Arrange the hoops in a 3x3 grid as shown. Line the wolves up at one end and the foxes at the other. They can only move from hoop to hoop.

2. The foxes are allowed to make the first move. The first fox moves into a hoop of their choice.

3. The first wolf may now move into a hoop of their choice at the opposite end of the grid.

4. Now the second fox may make their first move. They may NOT enter the game into the same hoop as the previous fox. The first fox may also now take their second move.

5. Next, the second wolf may make their first move. They may NOT enter the game into the same hoop as the previous wolf. The first wolf may also now make their second move.

6. The teams continue to cross their animals in this manner. Creatures are not allowed to use hoops used by their fellow animals in their previous move. If there are no free hoops for any creatures then a fight is deemed to have occurred and the challenge is failed!

Extension: The difficulty of the problem can be increased by increasing the size of the teams and reducing the number of hoops.

43 Team-building Activities for Key Stage 1
© Gavin Middlewood and Andrew Debenham

Lights out!

A power cut has hit your town and suddenly all the lights have gone out in your house. The bad news is that your baby brother, Joshua, is scared of the dark. He starts to cry. 'Can you fetch your torch so that we can have some light?' your mother asks. It is upstairs so you will need to tread carefully!

Instructions

1. The agility ladder/hoops should be set out to represent the stairs.

2. Each team should blindfold one person who will attempt to go upstairs (across the course).

3. The rest of the team must then communicate effectively with their blindfolded member so that they do not miss a stair (touch the equipment). If they do so they must return to the start.

4. After the blindfolded player has completed the activity, then another member of the team needs to attempt the task, and so on, until all pupils have had a turn.

Focus
Balance, communication
Number in group
2-5
Equipment
Agility ladders or hoops
Blindfolds
Aim
To transport each team along the ladder/hoops blindfolded and without touching the equipment.

Extension: Ladders/hoops set out in a curved line will make this activity harder.

Anthill attack

Why must ants and beetles always be falling out? It is the turn of the dung beetles to be angry this time, all because of something that some silly ant said about their homes being smelly! They are, in fact, so cross that they have decided to knock down the ant cities! It is the job of the soldier ants to stop the beetles' big boulders bashing down their hilly homes. If their aim is good then the day might yet be saved!

Instructions

1. First you will need to construct the ant city with a diamond formation of markers, each one topped with a tennis ball.

2. The beetles need to line up with their boulders (large balls). The ants are allowed to arrange themselves around the edges of the city armed with their beanbags.

3. On your command, the first beetle rolls his ball in an attempt to destroy an ant hill (dislodge one of the tennis balls from its holder). The ants must now decide when to throw their beanbags in an attempt to divert the boulder from its course. They should plan together where to stand and when to throw.

4. Once the boulder has stopped moving, the ants can retrieve their beanbags ready for the next attacking roll of the beetles.

5. Once all of the beetles have rolled, the turn is over. Children can now swap roles and ultimately compare scores.

Focus
Coordination
Number in group
2 teams of 3 or more
Equipment
9 cones/markers
9 tennis balls
Beanbags
Large balls
Aim
Beetle team: to knock the tennis balls from their markers using large balls.

Ant team: to stop the large balls from hitting their targets by diverting them with beanbags.

Extension: The targets can be made harder to hit by moving them further apart from each other.

43 Team-building Activities for Key Stage 1
© Gavin Middlewood and Andrew Debenham

The Easter bunnies

The Easter bunnies have been working far too hard this year in the land of Gazaban. NIBBLE, NIBBLE, HOP, HOP, CARRY HERE, CARRY THERE … their little paws are sore, sore, sore and quite frankly they just want to go to bed! However, they still have lots of eggs to deliver. Not only eggs in fact, but also iced lemon doughnuts and packets of mini chocolate eggs of all different colours. Now, Prince Larry (who has a giant sweet tooth and an even bigger dad!) has asked for something of every colour and every type for Easter morning. You are exhausted! How can you do as he asks without working too hard?

Focus
Problem-solving, coordination
Number in group
2-4
Equipment
Hoops
Beanbags
Small balls
Quoits
Aim
To transport the smallest number of items to their hoop, at the same time ensuring that all colours and object types have been collected.

Instructions

1. You will need to spread a large number of eggs (small balls), doughnuts (quoits) and packets of mini eggs (beanbags) around the playing area. These should be of a variety of colours.

2. Sort the bunnies (children) into groups and give each group a basket (hoop). This must be left in one place until all the objects needed have been collected.

3. Tell the bunnies that they must fill the basket with each colour and each item. You could inform them that they need to plan carefully as a 'winning basket' is likely to have very few items in. They should be given one minute's planning time.

4. One at a time the bunnies must jump with their feet together to retrieve their chosen object. They should use their knees to pick things up (their paws are far too sore to carry anything!).

Extension: Increasing the range of available colours will increase the complexity of the problem.

The burning rock

Bang! Crash! Aaaagh! All you can hear is screaming and all you can see is smoke. As you pop your head out of the window of your house, you see fire everywhere. It is coming from a giant burning rock that has fallen from space. You and your group of three friends must save the village from burning down by safely moving the rock and dropping it into the nearby ocean.

Focus
Problem-solving, cooperation
Number in group
4
Equipment
Skipping ropes
Quoits
Large/medium balls
Aim
To take the ball using only the equipment provided from one side of the playing area to the other.

Instructions

1. Give each group four skipping ropes and one quoit and tell them that they must use this equipment to move the burning rock (ball) to the ocean (the other side of the playing area). It cannot simply be dragged as this will damage the village.

2. Tell the groups that they will be able to choose one member with super-tough hands to lift the burning rock onto the quoit. After this point, no-one is allowed to touch the burning rock.

3. Give the groups time to plan how they will move the rock. They will need to build the equipment first.

4. The groups can then attempt to complete the task and take the rock to the ocean.

Hint: Several ropes will need to be used at the same time.

Extension: This can be attempted with three pupils in a group.

Transport cards

Photocopiable resource sheet (see page 25)

Colour sequence cards

Photocopiable resource sheet (see page 34)

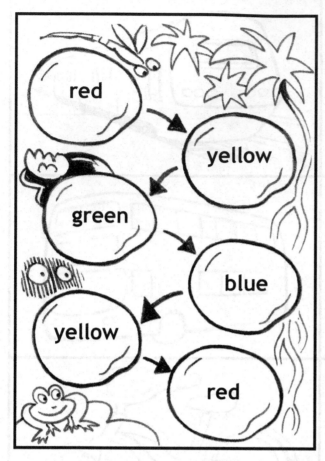

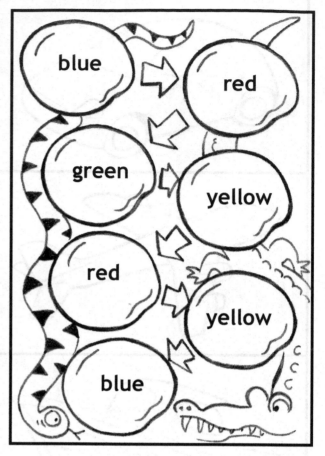

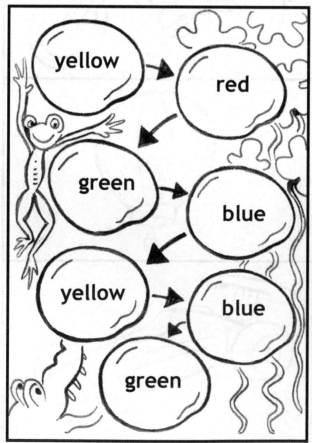

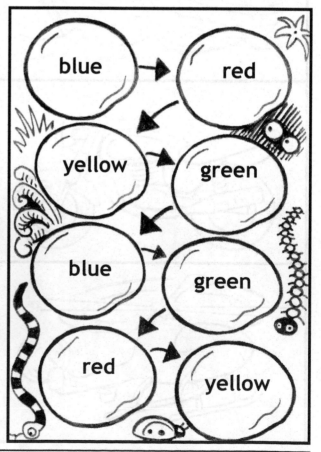

43 Team-building Activities for Key Stage 1
© Gavin Middlewood and Andrew Debenham

Spell cards

Photocopiable resource sheet (see page 36)

 1. Put the pea in the pod and the fig in the pig and do a jig!

 2. A bat's wing and a bell's ding and a bird's sing will do the finding!

 3. Hop and skip and jump and fall down in a lump!

 4. Up and down and round and round don't make a sound!

 1. Put a rat and a cat and a bat in a hat and shake them around and that will be that!

 2. Skip left skip right skip heavy skip light right through the night!

 3. One foot up then one foot down and then you pull your trousers down!

 4. Find a cow that is brown and big then poke it with a muddy twig!

 1. Take the eye of a bat and the tail of a rat then roll and turn and twist and burn to find the one for which you yearn!

 2. The finding spell is a binding spell so spell it all properly to do it really well!

Spanish words

Photocopiable resource sheet (see page 47)

casa house		**tesoro** treasure	
agua water		**cueva** cave	
playa beach		**roca** rock	
campo field		**piedra** stone	
colina hill		**arena** sand	
arbol tree		**pueblo** village	
coche car		**isla** island	
tienda shop		**cubo** bucket	

Lightning Source UK Ltd.
Milton Keynes UK
UKOW05f1417140118

316062UK00002B/10/P